Contents

Any words appearing in the text in bold, **like this**, are explained in the Glossary.

Animals in danger

giant panda

Bengal tiger

black rhino

All these animals are in danger.

All over the world, more than 10,000 animal **species** are in danger. Some are in danger because their home is being **destroyed**. Many are in danger because people hunt them.

Animals in Danger

MOUNTAIN GORILLA

Rod Theodorou

Heinemann
LIBRARY

www.heinemann.co.uk
Visit our website to find out more information about Heinemann Library books.

To order:

 Phone 44 (0) 1865 888066

 Send a fax to 44 (0) 1865 314091

 Visit the Heinemann Bookshop at www.heinemann.co.uk to browse our catalogue and order online.

First published in Great Britain by Heinemann Library,
Halley Court, Jordan Hill, Oxford OX2 8EJ,
a division of Reed Educational and Professional Publishing Ltd.
Heinemann is a registered trademark of Reed Educational and Professional Publishing Ltd.

OXFORD MELBOURNE AUCKLAND
JOHANNESBURG BLANTYRE GABORONE
IBADAN PORTSMOUTH (NH) USA CHICAGO

Designed by Ron Kamen
Illustrated by Dewi Morris/Robert Sydenham
Originated by Ambassador Litho ltd
Printed by South China Printing in Hong Kong/China

ISBN 0 431 13340 9 (hardback)   ISBN 0 431 13345 X (paperback)
05 04 03 02 01   05 04 03 02 01
10 9 8 7 6 5 4 3 2 1   10 9 8 7 6 5 4 3 2 1

British Library Cataloguing in Publication Data

Theodorou, Rod
  Mountain gorilla. – (Animals in danger) (Take-off!)
  1.Gorilla – Juvenile literature 2.Endangered species – Juvenile literature
  I.Title
  599.8'84

Acknowledgements
The publishers would like to thank the following for permission to reproduce photographs:
Ardea London: Adrian Warren pg.26; FLPA: pg.24, Gerard Lacz pg.4, Fritz Polking pg.4, Eichhorn Zingel pg.4, Phil Ward pg.5, pg.11, pg.14; ICCE: C & R Aveling pg.8; NHPA: Martin Harvey pg.13, pg.17; Oxford Scientific Films: Richard Packwood pg.9, Konrad Wolthe pg.12, pg.18, pg.21, Andrew Plumptre pg.15, pg.16, pg.22, M Austerman pg.20; Still Pictures: John Cancalosi pg.6, Michel Gunther pg.7, pg.23, Arnold Newman pg.19, Francois Pierrel pg.25, Mark Carwadine pg.27.

Cover photograph reproduced with permission of Oxford Scientific Films.

Our thanks to Sue Graves and Hilda Reed for their advice and expertise in the preparation of this book.

Every effort has been made to contact copyright holders of any material reproduced in this book. Any omissions will be rectified in subsequent printings if notice is given to the publishers.

Mountain gorillas like these are in danger of becoming extinct.

This book is about gorillas and why they are in danger. Gorillas will become **extinct** if people don't look after them.

Gorillas are among the most intelligent animals in the world.

What is a gorilla?

Gorillas are very big mammals.

Gorillas are huge **mammals**. There are three different types of gorilla. They are the western lowland, eastern lowland and mountain gorilla.

The mountain gorilla is the largest of all the gorillas.

The largest of all the gorillas is the mountain gorilla. It has a blacker face and bushier hair than the two other types of gorilla.

A **male** mountain gorilla can weigh up to 180 kilograms.

What do mountain gorillas look like?

Mountain gorillas have long arms, short legs and long black hair.

Mountain gorillas have long arms and short legs. Their hair is long and black. **Male** gorillas are twice as large as **female** gorillas.

A female gorilla can weigh up to 90 kilograms.

silver-grey hairs

Silverback gorillas like this one are very strong.

The biggest and oldest male in a gorilla family is called the 'silverback'. He is called silverback because the grey hairs in his back look silvery in the light.

Where do mountain gorillas live?

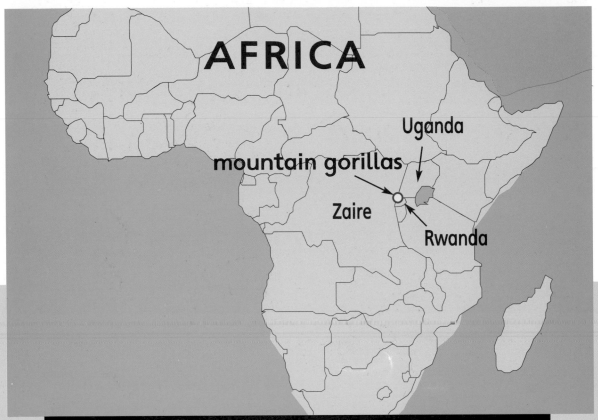

This map of Africa shows where mountain gorillas live.

Mountain gorillas live in three African countries called Uganda, Zaire and Rwanda. They live in misty forests high up in the mountains.

Mountain gorillas sometimes climb trees to find food.

Mountain gorillas spend most of their time living on the ground. They even sleep on the ground. Sometimes they climb trees to find food.

Gorillas mostly walk on all fours, using the knuckles of their hands and soles of their feet.

What do mountain gorillas eat?

This mountain gorilla is eating leaves and stems.

Mountain gorillas are **herbivores**. They eat leaves, fruit, berries and bamboo shoots. Sometimes they will also eat insects, snails and slugs.

Mountain gorillas use their large teeth and strong jaws to eat thick leaves and stems.

A mountain gorilla rests after eating.

Mountain gorillas spend half the day feeding or exploring and looking for new places to find food. The rest of the day is spent resting.

Mountain gorillas need to eat a lot of food to provide energy for their huge bodies.

Mountain gorilla babies

The silverback male stays with his family all the time.

silverback gorilla

Gorillas live in groups of about ten. There is always one big silverback **male**. He protects the group from predators. He stays with his family all the time and **mates** with the **females**.

mother gorilla

baby gorilla

The baby gorilla clings to its mother's chest.

Females usually have only one baby. It holds onto its mother's chest and drinks her milk. When it gets older, it rides on her back.

The baby gorilla is born 8 to 9 months after the male and female mate.

15

Looking after the baby

baby gorilla

mother gorilla

The baby gorilla stays close to its mother.

Baby gorillas stay close to their mothers for about three or four years. Other females look after the baby while its mother is feeding.

Gorillas are very good mothers.

adult female gorilla

baby gorilla

The baby gorillas in the group like to stay close to each other.

Gorilla babies grow very quickly. There are usually several babies in the group at one time. They like to play with each other and have pretend fights.

Gorillas do not like anyone staring at them. To them it means you want to fight!

Unusual mountain gorilla facts

mountain gorilla

nest

A mountain gorilla makes a nest to sleep in each evening.

A mountain gorilla:

- makes nests of grass and leaves
- makes a new nest each evening
- makes its nest on the ground or up a tree.

chest

hands

A gorilla beats its chest to scare a predator away.

A mountain gorilla:

- watches out for **predators** all the time
- stands up and beats its chest with its hands to scare predators away.

How many gorillas are there?

All gorilla species are protected by law.

Gorillas are **protected by law**. Even so, there are very few of them alive today. There are 32,000 western lowland gorillas and fewer than 5000 eastern lowland gorillas left.

Mountain gorillas are the most endangered.

Mountain gorillas are the most **endangered** of all the gorilla **species**. There are only 500 left today. There are no mountain gorillas in zoos or safari parks.

Why is the gorilla in danger?

Hunters are the biggest danger to gorillas.

hunters

People shoot gorillas and then cut off their heads, hands and feet to sell them as **trophies**. Some hunters shoot gorillas to eat their meat.

This gorilla has been caught in a trap meant for smaller animals.

Sometimes gorillas are caught in traps that hunters have set for smaller animals. Even if the gorilla escapes or is set free again, it may have been injured and might die.

Baby gorillas like this one are sometimes sold to zoos.

Sometimes hunters kill mother gorillas so they can take their babies. They sell the babies to zoos. Sometimes the whole gorilla family is killed, just so the hunter can steal the babies.

Gorillas need a **rainforest** habitat like this to be able to survive.

The **habitat** where gorillas live is being cut down and destroyed. The trees are sold for wood and the land is used for farming. Without the right habitat, the gorilla cannot survive.

How is the gorilla being helped?

These conservation workers look after the gorillas in their care.

Killing gorillas is now against the **law**.
Conservation groups such as the World Wide Fund
for Nature (WWF) are working to save the gorillas.
They try to stop **poachers** killing the gorillas.

Guards protect the gorillas from poachers.

Uganda, Zaire and Rwanda have places where the gorillas are **protected** by guards. Sadly, the poachers still kill many gorillas.

Tourists can visit these protected places to see the gorillas.

Mountain gorilla factfile

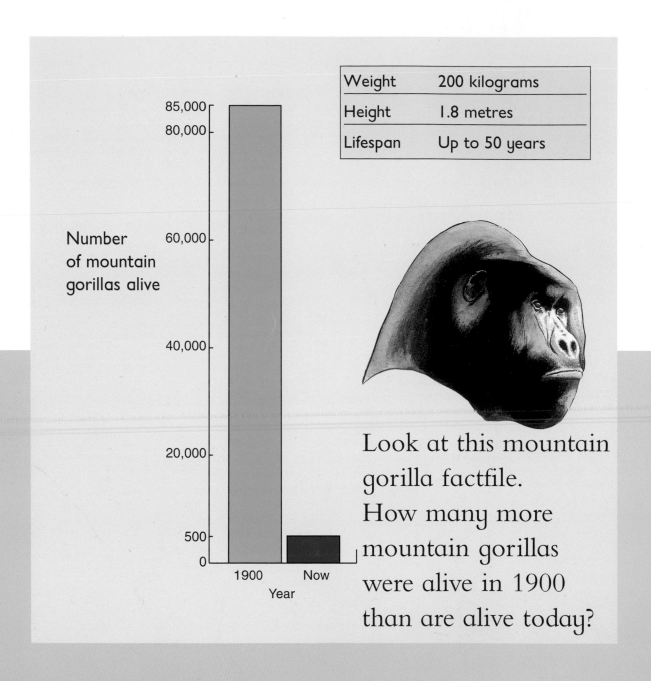

Weight	200 kilograms
Height	1.8 metres
Lifespan	Up to 50 years

Number of mountain gorillas alive

85,000
80,000
60,000
40,000
20,000
500
0

1900   Now
Year

Look at this mountain gorilla factfile. How many more mountain gorillas were alive in 1900 than are alive today?

World danger table

	Number that may have been alive 100 years ago	Number that may be alive today
Giant panda	65,000	650
Bengal tiger	100,000	4500
Blue whale	335,000	4000
Black rhino	1,000,000	2000
Florida manatee	75,000	1400

There are thousands of other animals in the world that are in danger of becoming **extinct**. This table shows some of these animals. How can you find out more about them?

Further reading, addresses and websites

Books

A Family of Gorillas, Animal Families series, Paul H. Burgel and Manfred Hartwig, A & C Black, 1990

Gorilla, Eyewitness Guides, Ian Redmond, Dorling Kindersley, 1995

The Atlas of Endangered Species, John A. Burton, David and Charles, 1991

The Mountain Gorilla, Melissa Kim, Hutchinson Children's Books, 1994

Vanishing Species, Green Issues series, Miles Barton, Franklin Watts, 1997

Organizations

Friends of the Earth:
UK – 26–28 Underwood Street, London N1 7JQ ☎ (020) 7490 1555
Australia – 312 Smith Street, Collingwood, Vic 3065 ☎ 03 9419 8700

Greenpeace:
UK – Canonbury Villas, London N1 2PN ☎ (020) 7865 8100
Australia – Level 4, 39 Liverpool Street, Sydney, NSW 2000 ☎ 02 9261 4666

WWF:
UK – Panda House, Weyside Park, Catteshall Lane, Godalming, Surrey GU7 1XR ☎ (01483) 426 444
Australia – Level 5, 725 George Street, Sydney, NSW 2000 ☎ 02 9281 5515

Useful websites

www.bbc.net
The BBC's animals site. Go to Animal Zone for information on all sorts of animals, including fun activities, the latest news, and links to programmes.

www.bornfree.org.uk
Virginia McKenna's site, which has the latest information on campaigns to save gorillas, tigers and other animals.

www.gorilla.org
The Gorilla Foundation's site, including the Koko for Kids feature.

www.defenders.org
The site of a conservation group dedicated to protecting animals and plants. Go to the Kids Planet site for games, fun activities, latest news and facts.

www.staffs.ac.uk
The Dian Fossey Gorilla Fund's site, dedicated to protecting the mountain gorillas of the Virungas.

www.wwf.org
The site of the World Wide Fund for Nature (WWF), the world's largest independent conservation organization. The WWF conserves wildlife and the natural environment for present and future generations.

Glossary

conservation	looking after animals, places or things so that they can continue to exist
destroyed	spoilt, broken or torn apart so it can't be used
endangered	in danger of dying out and becoming extinct
extinct	completely died out and can never live again
female	the opposite of a male, such as a girl or woman
habitat	home or place where something lives
herbivore	animal that eats plants but not meat
law	rule or something you have to do
male	the opposite of a female, such as a boy or man
mammals	warm-blooded animals, like humans, that feed on their mother's milk when they are young
mate	when a male and female come together to make babies
poacher	hunter who make money from hunting animals to sell parts of their bodies
predator	animal that hunts and kills other animals
protected	looked after, sometimes by law
protected by law	there are laws to make sure they are not harmed
rainforest	tropical forest that is very hot and damp
species	group of living things that are very similar
tourist	someone who visits a place for a holiday
trophy	souvenir or prize

Index